THE BANANAS DATING TEST

by
Joe Arthur
Illustrated by
B.K. Taylor

SCHOLASTIC INC.
New York Toronto London Auckland Sydney

DEDICATION
For Laura, who gladly did the field research, and Jenny, who watched from behind a chair.

Bananas dating test follows

ISBN 0-590-32161-7

12 11 10 9 8 7 6 5 4   7 8 9/8

Phony Table of Contents*

1. Dating: Then & Now
2. Dating: Now & Then
3. Going Out While You're Grounded
4. The Formal Invitation: How Informal Can It Be?
5. Proper Dress: Looking Casual At That Big Formal Dance
6. A Steady Date
7. An Unsteady Date
8. Selecting Her Flowers: For The Prom, For The Drive-In
9. Breaking Up's Really Not Very Hard To Do
10. Dutch Treat?
11. Belgian Treat?
12. Going Dutch On Belgian Waffles
13. First Dates
14. Repeating Your First Date And Getting It Right This Time
15. Being Stood Up
16. Being Sat Back Down
17. Good-Night Kiss?
18. Good-Riddance Kiss?
19. Choosing Your Blind Date
20. Double Dating
21. Double Crossing Your Double Date
22. Asking For A Date
23. Begging For A Date
24. Loving Gifts Of Distinction For Under A Quarter
25. Party Games: Post Office or United Parcel Service?

*Why bother with a real one? No one reads them anyway.

Introduction

This is a test! For the next 792 pages we're going to find out how much you don't know about dating and how poorly you compare with the rest of the nation. Sounds like fun, right?

Several months ago, while you were sound asleep, we passed out copies of *The BANANAS Dating Test and Survey* to a group of typical high school students. We got back surveys from a full 100%. That's because none of them was particularly hungry at the time. (Full-get it?!) And even though our sample of active daters was a small one, we always say that if your sample is made up of the right three people, a lot can be learned about people in general. (Especially since most of the people in our sample lived in General their entire lives.)

The BANANAS Dating Test and Survey consisted of 7,983 questions, none of which had right or wrong answers. Even so, 88% of the respondents were in the lower 100 percentile, and this included a shocking 29% of them in the bottom 29%. Eighty-eight percent forgot to put names on their papers. The remaining 64% didn't put names on their papers because they didn't know which papers were theirs — there weren't any names on them.

Before you begin comparing yourself with this typical group of American high school students, you'll need some special supplies: one #2 pencil, two #1 pencils, one ballpoint pen, one ballpoint pencil, one three-ring note-book, one hundred sheets of two-ring note-book paper, one paper punch, one protractor, one retractor, one compass, one sextant, one straight edge, one crooked edge, two cups of flour, a cup of sugar, a pinch of salt, and a whole handful of erasers.

Once you've assembled the necessary materials, turn to the first test and begin answering the questions. Be sure to keep the following tips in mind as you proceed:

- This is a time test. You have as much time to complete it as you need, so you'd better hurry up!
- If a question seems to have you stumped, don't waste precious minutes trying to figure it out. Go on back to the previous question which also had you stumped and work on *it* for a while.
- If you've read an item ten times or more and it still has you baffled, try reading it once from left to right. And turn the book so that the last line on every page is at the bottom.
- If you're taking this test with a group, and you get ideas about cheating, forget it! The person sitting on your left probably doesn't know any more of this stuff than you do. Try the person on your right.
- In a multiple choice type question that seems like all four choices are correct, the odds are pretty good you'll get it wrong.

Sharpen your protractor, pop a refill into your ruler, and turn to the first section of *The BANANAS Dating Test.*

The BANANAS Dating Readiness Test

Just because you can't tie your own shoes doesn't mean you're not ready for dating. All it means is you should stick to loafers. Besides, there are probably a hundred other good reasons why you're not ready. If it doesn't accomplish anything else, this test should prove it.

Part One: Multiple Guess

1. You find yourself talking with that good-looking girl who sits behind you in study hall. So she doesn't fall asleep or find out what a nerd you are, it would be best to steer the conversation around to
   a) how the only way anyone'd ever know she wears braces is if she opens her mouth.
   b) the many responsibilities of the linebacker in professional football.
   c) how beautiful that girl in the front row is.
2. Your mother is breathless with excitement when she yells, "There's a boy calling you!" You should:
   a) ask her just what it is he's calling you.
   b) jump up and down and scream, "I caught one! I caught one!"
   c) hide in the back of your closet so you'll

be sure nobody can possibly see that you're blushing.

3. You've had your eye on Clare Voiant for some time, but rumor has it she's already going steady with someone else. The best way to find out for sure is
   a) to follow her 24 hours a day for at least a month.
   b) tell her you're an official government census taker and you'll need the full names of her father, mother, brothers, sisters, and any steady boyfriends.
   c) put an announcement in your school's daily bulletin that there'll be an important meeting Tuesday after school in Room 204 of all the boys who are currently going steady with Clare Voiant.

4. One of the following is not an appropriate way to ask a girl for a date. Can you figure out which one it is?

a) "Geez, I really hope you can go because I'm getting tired of sitting here calling girls."

b) "Before you say anything, I want you to know it's not going to make one bit of difference so far as my seeing the movie is concerned. I can always go alone just as easily as I can go with you, and a whole lot cheaper!"

c) "I think it'd be really fun to go out together. Besides, I can win a dollar from Bill Kull who bet me you'd say no."

5. One of the following best describes a double date:
   a) a date with identical twins.
   b) a date with your clone.
   c) very rare—it's all you can do to get *one* date, let alone two.

6. An interesting transfer student catches your eye, and you've decided you'd like to go to the big dance with him. To make sure there're no mistakes, and he understands your interest in him, you should:
   a) write him a note in study hall asking if you can borrow his government notes, and tell him you'll return them when he picks you up Friday for the big dance.
   b) tell him you heard he's having a lot of trouble finding a date for the dance, and you'll be more than happy to help him find someone.
   c) ask him if he'd like you to take him on a tour of the building. The tour will start Friday evening in the gym, where they just happen to be holding the big dance.

7. It is proper for a girl to telephone a boy only
   a) if the boy doesn't have a phone.
   b) if she has a chaperone when dialing.
   c) if she wants to ask him out, ask him to go steady, or ask him if he'd like to get married.

8. Which one of the following would not be

an appropriate place to take a date after the Senior Prom?

a) the dog races.

b) the cat races.

c) a truck stop.

d) for a visit with your ex-girlfriend.

e) for an appointment with your ortho-dontist.

9. Going Dutch means

a) the couple wears wooden shoes.

b) she pays his way and he pays hers.

c) he's about broke.

10. Most etiquette books point out there's no one correct way to wear flowers. This means

a) no matter how you wear them you won't be correct.

b) the boy can pin the corsage on himself if he wants to.

c) if the guy is one of those clumsy types, it's perfectly all right to have him pin the flowers somewhere where he can't hurt you—like on the bottom of one shoe.

11. At one time, going steady with a person was a definite step toward getting mar-ried to that person. Today going steady means

a) the couple is one step closer to break-ing up.

b) a guaranteed date every weekend while you shop around for someone new.

c) you called the girl on Monday for a date on Friday, and it's already Tuesday and she still hasn't broken the date.

12. You've just been out on the worst date in
    your entire life. Now you're hurrying to
    get the front door unlocked and this to-
    tally despicable boy is actually asking you
    for a date next Saturday. You should say:
    a) "You've got to be kidding! I mean this
       was absolutely the worst date I've ever
       had in my entire life and I wouldn't go
       out with you again if you were the last
       boy on earth! Nothing personal, of
       course."
    b) "Don't call me, I'll call you."
    c) "Sure, what time will you pick me up?"

Answer Key:

Answer F was correct in nearly all cases. In fact, the number of times it wasn't the correct response you could count on the fingers and thumbs of both hands. Most of the time when F wasn't the correct answer, D, E, G, H, I, or J was.

Every time you put F as the correct answer, give yourself an F.

Every time you put A as the correct answer, give yourself a pat on the back.

Every time you left an item unanswered, give yourself 5 points.

Every time you stopped and said, "This is ridiculous!" give yourself 15 points.

Every time you put this book aside to do something constructive, subtract 25 points.

Figuring Out Your Final Grade

Add all the points you've earned to the ones you didn't earn, remembering to include your depreciating allowance and your mental age, then copy the score off your boy/girlfriend's test.

What Your Grade Means:

If you scored—

500 thru 300 . . . Nothing! Anyone who scores 300 or more points on a 150 point test is either a cheat or a fool. The fact that you're reading this book indicates you're probably the latter.

299 thru 200 . . . What you know about dating could be engraved on the head of a pin, and there'd be plenty room left for a reunion of leprechauns.

199 thru 50 . . . The only way you'll ever get a date is if they start putting them in boxes of cereal.

 49 thru -7 . . . This book is aimed right at you! So duck.

Who's Who & Who Are They Dating?

Remember how surprised everyone was when it got around that Sam Missel was going steady with Meg O'Fone? It seemed like such an unlikely match. He was studying to be a laboratory experiment; she was captain of the football team. Who can understand these things?

These highly in-depth profiles outline the personalities of students whose relationships have withstood the test of time. Some of these couples have been going together for as long as two weeks! Read through the profiles, then match up the right boy with the correct girl. You'll find the answers at the end of this section, right between notions and small appliances.

The Class President

In a school filled with jeans and T-shirts, the Class President is always wearing one of his four-piece suits, even during gym. He's been on the campaign trail since third grade, and the only time he won't stop whatever he's doing to shake hands is when he's shaking hands. He flashes a lot of teeth with that boyish grin of his—teeth that don't lose their sparkle even when he's lying through them—pledging no increase in the price of prom tickets.

Whenever the teacher is looking for someone to give an answer the Class President jumps right up and says, "I'm glad you asked that question!"

FAVORITE TOPIC OF CONVERSATION: Himself.

FAVORITE CLASS IN SCHOOL: Speech VI or any subject where he can stand up and talk.

HOBBY: Analyzing precinct voter breakdowns.

LAST BOOK READ: *How To Win Friends & Influence Elections* by Paul Aticks.

PET PEEVE: People who don't vote—for him.

WHERE HE MOST LIKES TO TAKE GIRLS ON DATES: Five-dollar-a-plate fund-raisers.

GOOD-NIGHT TECHNIQUE: Shakes hands, looks lovingly into the girl's eyes, steps forward, and shakes hands again.

HIS CAREER GOAL: To be president of the United States.

WHAT HE'LL PROBABLY END UP BEING: An actor.

The Prom Queen

Better than having her own charge accounts, she has Daddy's! She buys so many clothes, girls who've gone shopping after the Queen has made her rounds have found the stores closed. On days she's not wearing the very latest styles she's wearing something even newer.

A natural blonde (naturally), with soft blue eyes and soft blue contacts, she's a rare beauty, and it's the rare boy who gets to take her out.

In her entire life she's never broken a nail.

HER FAVORITE MUSIC: That background stuff they play in the Young Junior Status department at this simply divine little boutique where she practically lives.

FAVORITE CLASS IN SCHOOL: Consumer Shopping.

FAVORITE TV SHOW: *The Incredible Hulk*.

HOBBY: Blow-drying her hair.

FAVORITE TOPIC OF CONVERSATION: Which one of these lipsticks makes her look even *more* simply fantastic?

WHERE SHE MOST LIKES TO GO ON DATES: Just out for a quick quiche with the regulars at Chef Avec's; dancing under the stars at the Hotel Bif du Cheveau's Roof Pavilion; finally a romantic, early morning breakfast of crepe suzettes at that wonderful new spot, Suzette's Crepes.

PET PEEVE: She tells a boy to please stop telling her how incredibly beautiful she is, and he does.

GOOD-NIGHT TECHNIQUE: Just as her date's about to take her hand, she asks him to take her home.

HER CAREER GOAL: To become Mrs. Dwight Sanford Stunningham III.

WHAT SHE'LL PROBABLY END UP BEING: Mrs. Ralph Smith.

The Big Business Major

The Big Business Major was shifting for herself long before she took drivers' ed. She knows right where she's going—to the bank. She may look frazzled, but this poor thing is definitely not poor.

Students willing to grade papers for their teachers are a dime a dozen. The Big Business Major charges five-fifty an hour. Before school in the morning she's got two paper routes, an egg route, a milk route, and a diaper service; but whatever the product, they're all *bread* routes! At noon she's paid to referee food fights. That's right after she's tickled the plastics on the lunchroom cash register for a small percent of the action, *plus* half the day-old Twinkies, which she proceeds to sell after the lunch line closes. She's your no-nonsense, business-before-pleasure kind of gal who knows that if you want to dance, you've got to pay the piper. (Last week she started piping lessons.) Someday she could be rich, but right now she can buy and sell you ten times over. If she thought she could find a buyer, she would!

FAVORITE SONG: Theme from "Wall $treet Week."

FAVORITE CLASS IN SCHOOL: Work-Study program.

LAST BOOK READ: *How To Profit From The Coming End Of The World.*

FAVORITE TOPIC OF CONVERSATION: Exactly how much money per hour she's losing

while she's on this date, unless of course her escort would like to consider this modest, little, convertible decreasing-term life insurance policy she just happens to have in her purse. Along with $3,987.16 in mad money.

HOBBY: Serving as president and general manager of Term Papers Anonymous.

FAVORITE TV SHOW: *The Price Is Right.*

WHERE SHE MOST LIKES TO GO ON A DATE: To a party, especially if she's giving it, and the theme is Tupperware!

HER CAREER GOAL: To become an investment counselor.

WHAT SHE'LL PROBABLY END UP BEING: A guidance counselor.

The Slide Rule Champion

Everyone recognizes this person. He's the one with horn-rimmed glasses that are too heavy for him to lift. Physically he's so weak that when he wants to ask a girl out he has to have help lifting the phone receiver. But he's smart. Only a girl in the upper 3% of her class can afford to turn him down when he asks for a study date. He might not make her swoon, but he can sure make her grades rise.

Unfortunately he's extremely absent-minded. One time he'll ask a girl for a date and forget to pick her up, next time he'll arrive at the front door only to discover he forgot to ask her out. This really isn't much of a problem, though, because most of the time he for-

gets to do both.

At last year's sophomore prom he was the only fellow in the hall with a carnation *and* a calculator. Not only did he know the volume of the punch bowl to the nearest square root, he told a lot of people who really didn't care to know.

FAVORITE SUBJECT IN SCHOOL: Advanced Differential Calculus.

HOBBY: Advanced Differential Calculus.

FAVORITE TOPIC OF CONVERSATION: Most of the time it's the Pythagorean theorem, but if his date's a really clever conversationalist, she can get him going on the variations inherent in the dual binary system.

LAST BOOK READ: *Uber Die Von Molekular-kinetischen Theorie Die Warme Gefirderte Bewegung Von In Ruhdenden Flussigkeiten Supendienrten Teilchen.*

FAVORITE MUSIC: Humming. The kind nuclear reactors do.

WHERE HE'S MOST LIKELY TO TAKE A DATE: Some nice secluded spot under the stars, where he can get an unobstructed view of the solar system with his telescope.

GOOD-NIGHT TECHNIQUE: He slips his arm around her, whispering that they're merely going to test that silly old Third Law of Physics that says two bodies can't occupy the same space at the same time.

HIS CAREER GOAL: To do research for the Atomic Energy Commission.

WHAT HE'LL PROBABLY END UP BEING: A chemist for the State Horse Racing Commission.

The Class Clown

The Class Clown tries to steal a girl's heart

with his stolen jokes.

One of those jokes is calling a girl at 3 A.M. to invite her to a Come As You Are party. He's the guy who showed up for the freshman picnic dressed as an ant. A date with him can be a long, long evening—especially since he keeps setting his date's watch back. (What a card!) He doesn't really need a date. What he really wants is a straight man.

FAVORITE MUSIC: Slim Whitman.

LAST BOOK HE TELLS EVERYONE HE READ: *Die Von Der Molekularkinetischen Theorie Der Warme Geforderte Bewegung Von In Re-henden Flussigkeiten Supenrten Teilchen With The Wind.*

FAVORITE TV SHOW: *Guiding Light.*

FAVORITE CLASS: Any class with a substitute.

WHERE HE LIKES TO TAKE HIS DATES: On snipe hunts.

FAVORITE TOPIC OF CONVERSATION: Re-telling the story about the time he picked this number at random out of the phone book, called it, and asked the person who answered if his refrigerator was running, and he said "no."

PET PEEVE: People who can't take a joke.

GOOD-NIGHT TECHNIQUE: As soon as they hit the front steps he staggers, and grabs his chest. "It's my heart, Snookums! Quick, gimme some mouth-to-mouth resuscitation!"

HIS CAREER GOAL: To become the next great American humorist.

WHAT HE'LL PROBABLY END UP BEING: A dentist.

That Snoop Who Works In the Main Office

The guy who takes this girl out does so at his own risk. She works in the main office where she can sneak a peek at her date's entire school record. She knows all about the dead frog in Miss Duddy's lunchbox, who had the idea to glue Mr. Goodhart to his swivel chair, and how, the day before exam week started, every last copy of old lady Argyle's eight-page final ended up in the dumpster. In fact she knows everything everyone always wanted to know about everybody, but was afraid to ask!

It's a wonder anyone takes her out. The Snoop's last victim found himself standing in her living room while she introduced him to her parents as "the one we were laughing about the other night, the one with the National Achievement Test score that's the same as his age."

FAVORITE CLASS IN SCHOOL: Communications.

HOBBY: Gossiping.

LAST BOOK READ: Mr. Zinker's Grade Book.

FAVORITE TV SHOW: *Today* Show when Rona Barrett's on.

PET PEEVE: People with enough sense to keep their mouth shut.

HER CAREER GOAL: To be an operative for the CIA.

WHAT SHE'LL PROBABLY END UP BEING: A telephone operator.

That Quiet Boy Back in the Corner

He just might be the friendliest person in school, but since he never speaks to anyone, who would know? Nobody even knows his name. Nobody's sure if *he* even knows his name! His teachers point at him and say, "You there!"

Because he never says anything, it's widely assumed he's either incredibly intelligent or an escaped maniac. Unless of course he's a visitor from outer space. Most people lean toward the theory of high intelligence and take his silence to mean he's thinking. Watching him makes it clear, however, that if he's not thinking, he's not doing anything.

Actually this poor soul's so shy that he sits in corners away from windows because he's afraid of his own shadow. In kindergarten he was the only kid in the class who took a nap *underneath* the rug.

WHERE HE'S MOST LIKELY TO TAKE A DATE: Because he's much too shy to take a girl out, he'll probably try to take her in. It's his tough luck that most girls are too smart to be taken in.

LAST BOOK READ: *Learning To Live With Shyness* by Anonymous.

FAVORITE TOPIC OF CONVERSATION: How, when you get right down to it, there's nothing more to say.

FAVORITE SUBJECT IN SCHOOL: Silent Reading.

FAVORITE MUSIC: Enjoys listening to his collection of blank cassettes.

GOOD-NIGHT TECHNIQUE: He's much too shy to kiss a girl good-night. In fact he's too shy to even *say* good-night.

HIS CAREER GOAL: To see a little of the country first.

WHAT HE'LL PROBABLY END UP BEING: Rich.

The Athlete

He's strong as an ox and just about as smart. Chivalry's not dead with him, though no one doubts he's big enough to kill it.

Always eager to please his date, he doesn't stop at holding the door. He holds the whole car. And when he says he'll pick her up at eight — he'll *pick her up* at eight!

Over 99% of the places he goes with his dates are sporting events, so a girl should never take it personally if he invites her to the dog races. Another one of his ideas for a fun evening is letting his date act as his corner person while he participates in championship mud wrestling.

LAST BOOK READ: *The Hardy Boys in The Haunted Locker Room.*

FAVORITE TOPIC OF CONVERSATION: The big game last fall where he caught that spectacular field goal.

HOBBY: Push-ups, which he tends to do whenever he feels like it, no matter where he is. He did 206 at once last year, all in the time it took to announce and crown the Snow Princess at the Frostbite Fling.

FAVORITE TV SHOW: *Georgia Wrestling.*

FAVORITE MUSIC: "Notre Dame Fight Song."

GOOD-NIGHT TECHNIQUE: Just as his date thinks this record-holding weight lifter wants to press her to him, she finds he simply wants to bench-press her.

HIS CAREER GOAL: To be a wide receiver for Dallas.

WHAT HE'LL PROBABLY END UP BEING: In shipping & receiving.

Instructions: Now rate each type boy or girl, whichever seems appropriate, as a possible date FOR YOU! Use the following handy scale:

1. *NO!*
2. Not in a million years!
3. Only if I can keep my eyes closed and hold my nose.
4. It takes all kinds to make the world, but this person could start another planet.
5. Sure, if it's OK for me to wear a surgical mask.
6. Maybe, if Dan Rather interrupts with a news bulletin that the world's going to end in the next half hour.
7. How bad could it be? It couldn't be any worse than going to the dentist.

The Movie Date: Selecting The Right Film

One young man in *The BANANAS Dating Test and Survey* sample told us he lives in a small town that has only one theater, so it's pretty easy for him to decide what movie he's going to take his date to see. He flips a coin.

Naturally, the evening's main feature is the two of you, but that doesn't mean the planned entertainment shouldn't be just as spectacular. This test will help you put a little thought into picking out the right movie.

Important Questions To Consider:

1. What type of movie does she prefer? Talkies? Stories with plots? Love stories that make you want to cry? Love stories that make you want to throw up?
2. Does he like Disney movies with all those sweet little furry animals that speak better English than you do?
3. Or does he prefer movies where Jack Nicholson is a crazed maniac who takes a hatchet and chops furry animals up into dog food?
4. Did you ask her if she's seen the one

about the big gorilla who takes the girl to the top of the World Trade Center only to be turned away because he's not wearing a tie?

5. Did you hear the one about the zebra and the skydiver?

6. Is it really a good idea to take her to a movie where you risk being compared to Clint Eastwood or Burt Reynolds? Especially when *you're* paying for it?

7. What have those clowns got you haven't got? OK — but can you list twenty other things?

8. On the other hand, what are the chances that seeing Clint Eastwood or Burt Reynolds might put her in the mood for love?

9. Isn't there anything playing with *both* of them?

10. Or what about a movie starring Brooke Shields?

Movie Quiz:

The following movies were taken from actual newspaper listings. Place the number 1 beside your first choice, number 2 beside your second choice, number 3 beside your third. Then show the entire list to your girlfriend and let her decide.

_____ *Return From Which Mountain?*

_____ *The Zombies Walk Among Us Without Hall Passes*

_____ *Zombie In Detention*

_____ *Twice Is Once Too Often*

_____ *Dressed To Pester*

_____ *Dial J For Jaywalking*

_____ *Ordinary Animals*

_____ *Raiders Of The Lost And Found*

_____ *They Shoe Horses, Don't They?*

_____ *A Star Is Delivered*

_____ *Dragontweeker*

_____ *The Treasure Of The Sierra Club*

_____ *Clash Of The Munchkins*

_____ *One Flew Over The Cuckoo Clock*

_____ *Dracula Joins The Red Cross*

_____ *The Count Of Monte Hall*

_____ *Saturday Night Fever Blister*

_____ *The Phantom Of The Soap Opera*

_____ *The Bad News Bears Test The Free Agent Clause*

_____ *Herbie Gets Totaled*

_____ *The Attack Of The Killer Murderer*

_____ *Planet Of The Hamsters*

_____ *Comma*

_____ *Revenge Of The Pink Grapefruit*
_____ *Look Out For That Truck, Charlie Brown!*

The Correct Answer:

The teenagers we surveyed were virtually unanimous in wanting to see the new movie by the producer who gave us those unforgettable horror classics, *Beggar's Night* and *The Smog*. Their new one is entitled *You'll Just Die When You See What I Got You For Your Birthday.*

The Advantages and Disadvantages to Dating

If you're not highly experienced with dating, you might not realize that there are a lot of disadvantages. For example, remember the embarrassment you felt the night you took her to a first-class restaurant for dinner, and you couldn't pay the check because she'd forgotten her wallet?

According to *The BANANAS Dating Test's* sample, here are the Top Six Advantages & Disadvantages to Dating. Would you agree with our choices? Would you disagree? Would it make any difference?

Advantages	Disadvantages
1. You don't have to stay home on Friday nights and watch TV.	1. You can't stay home on Friday nights and watch TV.
2. Dating gives you the opportunity to actually use all that stuff you were taught about manners and etiquette.	2. Dating means you've got to actually use all that stuff you were taught about manners and etiquette.

3. There'll be no more nights out with the boys wandering around looking for something to do.

3. There'll be no more nights out with the boys wandering around looking for something to do.

4. When you get invited to the prom you'll get a beautiful corsage.

4. After you've been to the prom you'll need a painful tetanus shot because he pinned the corsage to your skin.

5. Your parents will stop worrying about whether you're popular.

5. Your parents will start bugging you about not spending enough time with your family.

6. You're no longer the one your friends are always having to fix up with dates.

6. Now you're the one all your friends are counting on to find them dates.

You've Got to Stop Meeting Her Parents Like This

According to *The BANANAS Dating Test and Survey* — next to worrying about chapped lips — meeting your date's parents and exchanging a few words without sounding like a total fool, a jerk, a nincompoop, or all three is the most frightening part of a date. The following is a list of actual quotations collected from high school students. Some of them are in extremely poor taste. Can you figure out which ones? In the meantime, watch what you say and remember not to talk with your mouth full, especially if that's your foot in it.

1. "Your *mother?!* I thought she was your *grand*mother!"
2. "How do you do, Dr. and Mrs. Zetts, I've heard so much about you. In fact, I think I heard my Dad say he's suing Dr. Zetts for malpractice. I guess that means now that I'm dating your daughter I'll not only see you socially, I'll see you in court!"
3. "I like the way you've decorated this place. You've proven that a person can make a highly interesting room out of junk that other people throw out."

4. "Gee, your daughter's talked about you so much that I feel like I already know you. Just this afternoon she was telling me how old-fashioned and stodgy you are. No offense, but I can't for the life of me see how anyone could think a couple of fourteen-year-olds are too young to get married."

5. "I want you to know I'm very fond of your daughter. I mean, if it weren't for her I wouldn't be passing algebra."

6. "Where're we going tonight? Well, most guys I know'll take their girls to some boring movie, and out for the usual hamburger and fries, then over to River Road for the most important part of the night, a little hugging and kissing. I thought we'd just skip all that and drive right out to River Road for the important stuff. Don't wait up!"

7. "I met your daughter in gym class. We were in the locker room and she'd forgotten her shower cap so I went down to the cafeteria and got her one of those plastic garbage bags."

8. "I've had my eye on Susan for several days now, and when six other girls said they couldn't go because they had to clean out their purses, I said to myself, 'What've you got to lose?'"

Review Questions

1. If you want to call that special girl and ask her for a date, you've got to get her number first, right? But, would you recognize it if you saw it? Pick out the girl's real number from the phony ones below:
   a) 296–36–5587
   b) 056–101–500–9
   c) 36–24–36
   d) 1–800–555–4276. Operators standing by.

2. If your life is turning into a soap opera, wouldn't it be a good idea if you and your boyfriend broke for a commercial?

3. You asked this girl to go out Friday night and she said yes, then yesterday she told you she's got a babysitting job she just couldn't turn down, but you're welcome to come along. Under the circumstances, aren't you entitled to half her pay if you go?

4. Seven boys have asked you to go to the last big dance of the school year, the Humidity Hop. The problem is you really like them all and you don't want to hurt anyone's feelings. Is there anything wrong with telling all of them yes?

5. Since first dates are always so awkward, is there any reason you can't just skip the first date altogether and go right on to the second one?

6. Will she forgive you for constantly stepping on her feet at the big dance if you tell her it's because you worship the ground she walks on?

Mind Your Manners — Everyone Else Does: The BANANAS Dating Etiquette Test

Do you know the correct way to act in a given situation? Have you been given many situations? Could you give us one? Our situation is hopeless!

Part One: Multiple Guess

1. Millions have seen the picture of Queen Elizabeth I stepping over a cloak put down by Sir Walter Raleigh. He put the cloak down because
   a) it wasn't his cloak — he'd borrowed it.
   b) he was trying to invent chivalry but invented dry cleaning instead.
   c) he didn't put it down — nobody ever heard him say anything insulting about the cloak!
2. If the best tickets a boy could afford for a concert are in row ZZZ in the third balcony, the least offensive thing his date can say is:
   a) "Which direction's the stage?"
   b) "I hope they're wearing football jerseys, because without numbers we'll never be able to tell who's who."
   c) "Hey, don't worry about it! I can see

really well up here. It's down there I can't see a thing."

   d) "Do you have a handkerchief? I think I'm getting a nosebleed."

3. The finger bowl . . .

   a) should be well manicured and match the color of the lipstick.

   b) should be no closer than six inches to the foot bowl.

   c) was won last New Year's Day by Slippery Rock, 35-6, over Ohio State.

4. You see three forks beside your plate. This means

   a) two people at your table don't have forks.

   b) the dessert's not going to be Jell-O.

   c) there's no way to stay on your diet tonight.

5. You're on a double date at the indoor Tivoli Twin Filmplex. Which is the proper seating arrangement?

   a) Boy/Boy/Girl/Aisle/Girl/Stranger/Stranger/Weirdo

   b) Girl/Girl/Boy/Boy/Stranger/Stranger/Creep/Aisle

   c) Stranger/Girl/Stranger/Aisle/Girl/Stranger/Aisle/Boy/Boy

   d) Stranger/Girl/Masher/Creep/Weirdo/Girl/Mass Murderer/Aisle

   e) Girl/Usher/Girl/Boy/Usherette/Popcorn Seller/Projectionist

6. If the transportation the boy is providing for the evening is the city bus, proper etiquette requires

a) the girl to stand in the aisle so she won't wrinkle her outfit.
b) the girl to have the correct change only after 6 P.M. and on weekends.
c) that you select a bus the way you select a fine wine — sniff the diesel fumes until you find a bus with the right bouquet and character.

7. There are two spoons on the left side of your place setting. This means
a) the first course is soup and so is the second course.
b) you'll be dining on strained steak.
c) you're in the wrong banquet hall! This is the one for the A.A.P.F.T. — the American Association of People With False Teeth.

8. If the girl's having a truly dreadful time on her first date with a boy, it is entirely acceptable for her to
a) take out a book and start reading.

b) go to the nearest library to borrow a book and start reading.

c) stuff cotton in both ears and put on a sleep mask.

d) borrow 20¢ from him to go call that boy she wishes now she hadn't turned down.

9. He's invited you to the Junior Prom. You should wear

a) some designer's jeans.

b) your own jeans.

c) a coat and tie.

d) a long dress, a long coat, and long-johns.

10. If the boy hasn't told you specifically where you're going on your date this Friday night, you should dress

a) up.

b) down.

c) at home before he calls for you.

d) in a layered look and hope that one of the layers will be appropriate for wherever you're going.

11. You're at one of those restaurants that won't admit people unless they're wearing a coat and tie. You don't have a coat and tie. The best thing to do is

a) try to borrow a coat and tie from your boyfriend.

b) borrow a ballpoint pen and draw them on your tank top.

c) turn around and go where all they require is what you're already wearing — a shirt and shoes.

Part Two: True-False

Instructions: Put a T next to all true statements; put an F next to all false statements.

1. If your girl invites you to her home for Thanksgiving dinner, you ought to be at least as well-dressed as the turkey.
2. Just as a boy should be sure to match his brown leather watchband with a brown leather wallet and brown shoes, he should match a gold flexible band with gold-tone shoes and a brass wallet.
3. According to fashion experts, the reason a young man's necktie and socks must match so closely is so he can wear them interchangeably.
4. Once again, this year it is definitely NOT fashionable for the boy to have empty pockets.
5. At a restaurant, if you know from experience you don't like the house dressing on your salad, there's absolutely nothing wrong with ordering the garage dressing.
6. When a gentleman orders for his companion in a restaurant, this is just his way of saying, "I want you to know, darling, I'm not made out of money."
7. Proper etiquette requires that just as the boy holds the door for the girl when they enter a bowling alley, he should also hold her bowling ball for her until after she's released it down the lane toward the pins.
8. If the boy only has enough money for one

admission to the drive-in movie, it is a basic requirement of etiquette that he provide his date with a tarpaulin so she won't get her clothes too dirty hiding in the trunk.

9. The only acceptable reason for a girl to sit close to her date at a drive-in movie is to hear the speaker better.

10. It would be a really serious breach of etiquette for a girl who came to the drive-in movie with her date not to offer to switch seats with the girl in the back seat — so the guys can sit together and talk about cars, football, and women.

11. At a dance if someone goes over to the chaperones and speaks to them, the chaperones will appreciate this gesture, but everyone else will start asking who's getting squealed on and for what.

12. When you introduce your date to someone, you should include her name and something personal and complimentary about her. For example, "This is Linda. Her feet are so tiny, when we were horsing around the other day and she gave me one of her shoes to try on, I could only get five toes and my heel in it."

Part Three: For Boys Only

Instructions: Register your level of thoughtlessness for each of the following situations. Don't cheat unless the person assigned to proctor this test leaves the room.

Always	You Bet!	Do Birds Fly?	
[ ]	[ ]	[ ]	1. I call on my date at her door — the door to her room.
[ ]	[ ]	[ ]	2. Because I know how much her parents worry about her, I wait until we're out the front door before asking my date if she'd like to run away with me to Kentucky.
[ ]	[ ]	[ ]	3. I try very hard not to dominate the conversation, and make an effort to include her in my monologue.
[ ]	[ ]	[ ]	4. I dress in clothing appropriate to the occasion and usually wear shoes.
[ ]	[ ]	[ ]	5. Whenever I ask a girl out on a date, I always give her specific information, such as: "I'll pick you up Friday."

Part Four: For Girls Only

Instructions: Girls, now it's your turn. Check off the statement that best describes your dating behavior.

Not Likely	Never	You Got to be Kidding!	
[ ]	[ ]	[ ]	1. When a boy's thoughtful enough to ask me out in advance, I'm thoughtful enough to give him a definite maybe.
[ ]	[ ]	[ ]	2. If my date gives me a choice of restaurants, I always choose the expensive one so he'll know I have taste.
[ ]	[ ]	[ ]	3. I try to be on time so the boy doesn't get caught in an embarrassing conversation with my parents for more than a half-hour.
[ ]	[ ]	[ ]	4. I try to find out what he's interested in — so I can talk about that stupid, boring stuff.
[ ]	[ ]	[ ]	5. Neatness counts, especially on a date, so I always remember to tell him how really neat I think I am.

Letters from Homes

Dear BANANAS Dating Test:
I've already taken more than half the tests in this book and my average is only 38. Even if I get hundreds on all the rest of them, I figure the highest grade I can possibly get's a 57. I'm not sure because people tell me my math's even worse than my dating.

Confused

Dear Confused:
They're right.

Dear BANANAS Dating Test:
Before I started reading this stupid book, the biggest problem in my life was how could I improve myself so girls can stand me. Now that I'm failing all these tests, the biggest problem in my life is how am I ever going to be able to stand myself?

Disgusted

Dear Disgusted:
We couldn't even stand to read your letter.

Dear BANANAS Dating Test:
I just got a letter saying I'm going to be sued by my girlfriend's father's lawyer,

because I still have her 8½-by-11 full-color school photo. The reason I haven't returned it is I still love her, and I always will. I want to keep the picture right next to my pet guinea pig's cage as a priceless reminder of when we were deeply in love, and she went out with me once. I admit I took it off her wall, and I broke a really expensive lamp doing it, but I just had to have her picture because she's the only girl I'll ever love — especially if I get sent to detention home.

Prisoner of Love

Dear Prisoner:

Save a few of these tests so you'll have something to do while you're locked in the slammer.

Dear BANANAS Dating Test:

Thanks a lot, you creeps! My girlfriend got higher grades on all the tests in this book than I did, and now she teases me all the time about how stupid I am. You started all this trouble! Do you have any suggestions?

Humiliated

Dear Humiliated:

We suggest your girlfriend find herself a smarter boyfriend.

Dating Then & Now — Are You Up To Date?

Part One: Dating Time Line

Instructions: Arrange the following list of actual dating milestones in correct chronological order.

_____ 1.

_____ 2.

_____ 3.

_____ 4.

_____ 4.

_____ 5.

_____ 6.

_____ 8.

_____ 9.

_____10.

_____11.

_____12.

_____11.

_____13.

_____13.

A. The first ice cream social.

B. The second ice cream social.

C. The first frozen yogurt social.

D. The first time a boy told his girl his car had run out of gas.

E. The first time a boy took a girl out on a buggy ride and told her he'd forgotten to feed the horse.

F. The first game of Spin The Bottle with a loaded bottle.

G. The first game of Twister with a rigged mat.

H. The first time a father let his son have the keys to the car.

I. The first time a father let his son have the car, too.

J. The first time a girl couldn't go out because she had to wash her hair. (Clue: It's later on the same day the Earth was created!)

Part Two: True-False

Instructions: If you don't know how to take a True-False test by now, it's not very likely we can teach you here.

1. As recently as the 1890s it was not considered appropriate for a girl to call a boy unless she used a phone.
2. The average high school couple is now allowed to stay out until midnight, and this average has risen a half-hour every five years. This means that in 1955 a typical couple out on a date had to be home two full hours before they left.
3. During the 1950s it was a fashion requirement to wear heavy, starched petticoats called crinolines, even on an informal date, and the girl was expected to get all dressed up, too.

Say What?

Do you know how to ask for a date? If you were being asked out on one, would you know it? Do you know what day it is? We didn't think so. This test won't help a bit, but it'll fill in a little time before you once again have to face the horrible reality of your social life.

Instructions: Place an A beside those things that are ACCEPTABLE to say when asking for a date, and an A beside those items you ought to AVOID.

_____ 1. "My name's Harold. How's about you and me getting together this weekend for a little kissy face?"

_____ 2. "And if you can't go, what's your sister look like?"

_____ 3. "Tell you what, Clare, I'll make you a deal. You agree to go out with me, and I'll agree to drive and even pay your way!"

_____ 4. "I think we can avoid our first big fight if you just say yes."

_____ 5. "There's a really scary horror movie at the Ravioli: *Godzilla Goes Hollywood*. Would you like to go along and hold my hand?"

_____ 6. "Hey, it's no big deal, really! If you don't want to go I'll just stay home by myself and watch TV, pop some corn, kill myself."

_____ 7. "Now, before you say anything, I know you haven't got anything better to do, because I've been asking around."

_____ 8. "Hey, I already told my best friend we'd double, and I never go back on my word. You've just *got* to go out with me, and you've got to *drive!*"

_____ 9. "Believe me, if you don't want to go out with me, I won't be offended, I'll understand. *I* wouldn't even go out with me!"

_____10. "I don't know, I'm sort of, well, scared asking you this, I mean since you're used to going out with a different type of person and all, but I'd really like to take you to the movies Friday night — that is if you don't mind dating someone with a superior intellect."

_____11. "How about you and me going out sometime? Some time tonight!"

_____12. "You haven't got a date, I haven't got a date, what've either of us got to lose? Just say yes — if it turns out to be a disaster, I promise, wherever we happen to be, I'll just stop the car and you can get out."

Excuses for the Girl Who Has Everything — Including a Boy She Doesn't Like Asking Her for a Date

Instructions: Using a check mark [✔] check only those excuses you might try — or have already tried — when you don't want to go out with that nerd on the other end of the phone. Then go back down the list and place a check mark [✔] beside all the stupid ones you wouldn't even think of trying.

_____ 1. "It's really nice of you to ask, but I never go out on weekends."

_____ 2. "I can't. My allowance is gone and I've only got enough eye shadow left for one eye."

_____ 3. "I'm going to give myself a permanent."

_____ 4. "I'm going to give myself a temporary."

_____ 5. "I told Mom weeks ago I'd go to the shopping center with her to get fitted for some new barrettes."

_____ 6. "Gee, I really wish I could, but I've got to darn my darn socks."

_____ 7. "Saturday night's the night I promised Mom I'd teach my little sister how to defrost orange juice."

_____ 8. "I'd love to go out with you, but my

Mom's an astrophysicist and she was telling me the other day that the world and everything in it's going to be blown to smithereens someday, so what's the point?"

_____ 9. "I'd like to, I really would, but I want to stay home in case the phone rings and someone interesting calls."

_____10. "I probably shouldn't be making any dates, Lester, since I'm planning on doing something in the next couple days that's bound to get me grounded."

_____11. "Friday night's out. That's the night I take my tropical fish to obedience school."

_____12. "Eight o'clock? Eight o'clock's fine. The only thing is, eight o'clock's the time my parents want me home."

Excuses for the Boy

Instructions: Let's say it's Turnabout Dance time and you find yourself on the other side of the fence. Check the excuses below that you think might help you get out of going out — without going out of your mind.

_____ 1. "I've got to wash my car."

_____ 2. "I've got to wax my car."

_____ 3. "I've got to wash my hair."

_____ 4. "I've got to wax my hair."

_____ 5. "I've got to wash my face."

_____ 6. "I've got to wash my socks. I washed my face last week."

_____ 7. "I won't dance, don't ask me."

_____ 8. "Sure, it'll be fun. The only thing is I'm in training, and Coach Blatt says I have to either walk or run everywhere I go *and* he wants me home at seven-thirty every night!"

_____ 9. "Well, I don't know if I should make any plans. I feel pretty good right now, but my temperature's already 98.6 and I figure if it doesn't drop, the only way it can go is up."

_____10. "I've got to change the battery in our smoke detector."

The Language of Love — A Chart with Heart

The BANANAS Dating Test and Survey was amazed to find out that love has a language all its own. (We were also amazed to find out that Albania has a language all its own, but that's another story.)

Check the chart below and find out what your dates *really* mean.

Puppy Love	Occurs when a girl gives it her best shot but still can't break up a boy and his dog.
True Love	The only guy who called and asked her for a date to the big dance.
Just Friends	How she feels about the guy who called to ask her for a date to the big dance the morning after the big dance.
Crush	What he did to her while he was kissing her good-night because he was so nervous.

Relationship	A couple that has been dating steadily for over a year, and they're both desperately looking around for someone new.
Being Used	Not being new.
Parking	What you do with the car while you're inside the theater watching a movie.
Feed Her a Line	Cheaper than feeding her dinner.

Don't Kiss Your Chance for a Good-Night Kiss Good-bye

The BANANAS Kissing Test

Kissing, or osculating as most young moderns call it, is as basic a part of dating as not knowing what to say. How will you rate in the great lipstakes? Take the BANANAS Kissing Test and find out.

Part One: Multiple Guess

Instructions: The best results from kissing tests are generally those obtained in sessions conducted under ideal laboratory conditions. But those of you who don't have a laboratory can pick up a pencil and take this test right where you are — nowhere!

1. When a boy's trying to kiss a girl good-night, under no circumstances should he say:
   a) "What d'ya mean you won't let me kiss you good-night?! The word around school is when you dated Henry Penry you let him kiss you any time he felt like it!"
   b) "Could you have your parents turn the front porch light on? I bet my friends

a dollar if they drove by your house about this time tonight they'd see me kissing the highly popular Sharon Smith!"

c) "I think we can go ahead and kiss — I don't think my measles are contagious anymore!"

d) "I don't usually insist on a good-night kiss on the first date, but it did cost me a little extra tonight because you wanted cheese on your pizza!"

2. If a girl wants a good-night kiss, under no circumstances should she say:

a) "Would you like a breath mint?"

b) "This will be a real challange for you, because I was at the dentist all day long and the Novocain hasn't worn off. You see I had root canal. They drilled down into a rotted putrid nerve and . . . "

c) "Now, so we don't have one of those embarassing, awkward moments, my experience has taught me the girl should tilt her head exactly 48.3 degrees to the left, and the boy should tip his a complementary angle to the right. Are there any questions?"

3. When it's finally clear she won't let you kiss her good-night, you shouldn't necessarily think it's because she doesn't like you. All it probably means is

a) she's got a weak rubber band on her braces and she's afraid it might snap during a kiss and injure you.

b) she's saving her kisses for that one great love, or at least for someone she can stand.

c) she's one of those preventive health nuts who wouldn't think of drinking out of the same glass you use, so naturally she's not about to take a chance on picking up even more germs from something as frivolous as a kiss!

4. When a young couple in love kiss good-night on her front porch, quite often both will say they heard bells ringing. Usually this is just a figure of speech, but if they really *do* hear bells, it means

a) he's got her pressed up against the doorbell.

b) there's a rival on the phone right this minute, probably calling to ask her for a date.

5. When the boy's two feet taller than the girl he's about to kiss good-night, the best way to handle this is

a) for him to pick her up and hold her at lip level.

b) for her to climb up on the porch railing.

c) if he had a shovel he could dig a hole to stand in, but since he doesn't — and they're at *her* house — she should hoist herself up using a block and tackle attached to a sky hook.

6. When the girl's a mere two feet taller than the boy, the best way to handle this one is

a) for the girl to build up his ego by telling him, "You're just the cutest little thing!

You remind me of my baby brother!"

b) tell him to throw you a kiss, but if he can't do that, suggest that he try launching one.

c) move the location of the good-night kiss from the front porch to the garage where there's a step ladder.

7. Which of the following highly important rules governing the good-night kiss is the most important rule of all?

a) Don't burp.

b) Don't drool.

c) Don't giggle.

d) Don't let go, no matter what!

Part Two: Essay Section

Instructions: Write thoughtful answers to these thoughtful problems that have been carefully selected for those who haven't thought much about kissing.

1. In many parts of the country it's not considered appropriate behavior for two people to kiss in public. What about one person?

2. Many experts in the field of kissology believe the most romatic kiss of all is one where the boy gently brushes the girl's lips. What kind of brush should he use?

3. Should it happen that her father comes storming through the door while you're in the middle of a good-night kiss, how can you make him believe you when you tell

him you've got a committee report to give next week in health, and you two were simply practicing your life-saving techniques?

5. If she invites you in after your date, puts some soft music on the stereo, turns the lights down low, and sits next to you on the couch, could this possibly mean you should take out your English book because you're finally going to learn how to diagram a sentence?

Part Three: Reading Comprehension

Instructions: The following steps are characteristic of the properly executed good-night kiss. Read down the list then pick out the one or ones that is/are/was/were/would have been/should have been misplaced. Draw a Cupid-style arrow/arrows from where it/they is/are but shouldn't be, to where it/they ought to be but isn't/aren't.

The Boy's Moves . . .

1. As they approach her front door he says, "Gee, it's still early, you don't have to be in for another fifty seconds."

The Girl's Responses . . .

1. As they approach her front door she removes her house key and a small can of mace.

2. Leading with his left foot, he takes one step toward her.

3. He raises his right arm until it's doing a perfect imitation of a cobra poised to strike.

4. He speaks softly to reassure her: "Isn't this a beautiful night, so cool."

5. He slips an arm around her waist.

6. Slipping another arm around her, he says, "I'm right here, I'll protect you!"

7. "What a sense of humor! I love a girl who likes to kid!" He moves a little closer.

2. Stepping back with her right foot, she steps back with her left foot, too.

3. She braces herself then turns the spray can so it's aimed right at his beady little eyes.

4. She says, "Do you mind if I open a door? It's getting close out here."

5. She says, *"What was that?! Who's back there?!"*

6. She says, "Yes, but who's going to protect me from you?"

7. "Who's kidding?" She tries to move a little closer too — to the door.

8. At the same time he's trying to outflank her, he's also sweeping her off her feet, and turning her, so he's placed himself between her and her front door.

9. "Have I told you lately that I think you're wonderful?" he asks her.

10. He asks, "Are you ready?"

11. His goal, which is her lips, is now only inches away. He tilts his head to the right, being careful to avert his nose exactly 17° off center so as to avoid an embarrassing collision.

8. Not only does she see her route of escape's been cut off, she's so dizzy from being swept off her feet she keeps trying to use her house key to unlock the shrubbery.

9. "Have I told you lately that my brother's a black belt in karate?" she asks him.

10. She answers, "NO!"

11. He's backed her head up against one of the posts supporting the front porch roof, but she has just enough room to twist her head at least 32° left to avoid contact with his lips.

12. He says, "OK, baby, pucker up!"

13. He says, "That's going to change! You'll learn to love me!"

14. He slips another arm around her and lowers his lips in her direction, saying, "Hang onto your socks, baby!"

15. His lips brush her hair, and he plants one first-class smacker on the front porch post!

12. She says, "But I hardly know you!"

13. She says, "You better not count on it. I can't even learn math."

14. She sidesteps right, allemandes left.

15. "Good-*night!*" she says as she slips out of his grasp and runs through the front door her mother has opened.

Letters From Homes

Dear BANANAS Dating Test:

I'm the only person I know who has to be home by 9:30 on weekends. Everybody else gets to stay out until 12 or 12:30. I don't think that's fair at all, but that's not the problem. My problem is no one ever asks me out anyway. Is there anything I can do to change this?

Stuck

Dear Stuck:

We can't think of anything.

Dear BANANAS Dating Test:

I'm really disgusted with my boyfriend. For some strange reason he never kisses me on the lips, only on the cheek. I'm too embarrassed to talk to him about it, and I'm getting madder by the minute! I'm afraid I might just snap one of these nights and I'll do something to hurt him. What should I do?

Frustrated

Dear Frustrated:

Turn the other cheek.

Dear BANANAS Dating Test:

Last week I approached this girl I really like in the lunchroom, and she just turned and walked away. Then I called her on the phone and she hung up on me. I sent her a note in class yesterday and she turned me in to the teacher. Do you think she's trying to tell me something?

                    Rejected

Dear Rejected:

No.

A Close Look At Blind Dates

Instructions: This test should be completed only in a realistic, simulated blind date environment. Get a couple of sharpened pencils and a blindfold.

Part One: Multiple Guess

1. Most blind dates are preferable to
   a) staying home alone.
   b) going out with your sister.
   c) being made to clean your room.
   d) none of the above.
2. When you set up the blind date, you said you'd wear a red rose so he'd know who you are, but now that you see him coming, one look is enough to know this is all a big mistake. You should
   a) eat your rose.
   b) tell him he must be color blind, your rose is blue.
   c) put the stem of the rose between your teeth and start stomping around like a Spanish flamenco dancer.
3. You're out on a blind date and it's pretty clear the person isn't very impressed with you. You should

a) try a little harder, maybe even pay for the milkshakes since she paid for the movie.

b) tell her even though you know she doesn't think much of you now, you'll ask her again after the two of you have spent three hours admiring your frog collection.

c) shrug it off, the way she did when you hit her with that water balloon (you big kidder, you!)

4. You're not too thrilled, but your blind date actually seems to be having a pretty good time. You should

a) pinch him to see if he's dreaming.

b) realize it's quite obvious why he's having such a great time and tear him away from his fourth banana split.

c) ask him if he'd like to go out next week and when he says yes, tell him you'll fix him up with a friend of yours who likes blind dates, too.

5. You're on a blind double date and you kind of like the girl your best friend is with, and it's obvious he's stuck on the one you're stuck with. The best solution is

a) to switch identities. You become your best friend and he turns into you!

b) next time pick girls neither one of you likes so there won't be any petty jealousy or bickering.

c) you and your best friend should spend the evening together, and the girls can do what they want.

6. When your best friend got you fixed up

with this blind date, she told you he was going to take you out to Wilderness Trails for a picnic in the great outdoors. Now, he shows up on your porch dressed in a tuxedo. You should

a) tell him to take a hike, since that's what you'd expected anyway.

b) tell him to hurry if he expects to get a choice spot to spread out your blanket and picnic lunch on the dance floor.

c) tell him you'll just be a minute, you didn't realize the picnic was formal.

7. Your blind date is pulling into the back row at the drive-in movie. Your best move would be

a) to point out how absolutely filthy his windshield is, and tell him you'll be able to see the movie better if you could just sit on the hood.

b) tell him your Dad's a geologist, and he told you never to come near this drive-in — it's built right on top of the intersection of two totally unstable faults.

c) ask him if he'll loan you a pencil and leave the light on because you've got to write a review of this movie for journalism class.

8. It's late, you're standing on the front porch with your blind date, and he's actually asking if you'd mind if he kisses you goodnight. You hardly know the fellow, so you should say

a) "Over my dead body!"

b) "Over *your* dead body!"

c) "Over there in the shadows!"

Part Two: True or False or What?

Instructions: If it comes down to a choice, write in T or F.

1. If a young couple truly enjoys each other's company, it is totally acceptable for them to have more than one blind date with each other.

2. Back in olden times the term blind date meant you didn't have any idea what day the fellow would show up to take you out.

3. The English words *blind date* come from the Latin root meaning *desperate.*

4. Studies show that given a choice between going out on a blind date or being shot at sunrise, most people will set their alarms for 5:30 A.M.

5. The type of blind date that's usually considered the most fun is the kind where both the boy and the girl not only haven't met each other before, but don't even know each other.

6. Experts agree that everyone should have at least one blind date so they'll fully understand the worst that life has to offer.

7. Most states now have laws stating that anyone who's been fixed up with more than ten blind dates in less than one calendar year should carry a warning label from the Surgeon General.

8. Recent scientific polling indicates that the best night of the week for a blind date is the night you can't get a regular one.

Grounds for Breaking Up

Let's say you've been going with someone for a good long time now, in fact, the longest you've ever gone with anyone — three whole weeks — but it's obvious the thrill is gone. Like it or not, you can't just break up. You've got to have specific grounds. According to *The BANANAS Dating Test and Survey* not every state recognizes every one of the following grounds for breaking up. And some states don't recognize any of them. But we're pretty sure you will. Check the ones that apply to your dating partner, then get right on the phone and start a fight.

_____ 1. Her idea of holding hands is keeping them folded in her lap.

_____ 2. When you two kiss, he causes such suction, your ears pop.

_____ 3. You told him if he really loved you he'd give you a ring, so after you got in last night he telephoned.

_____ 4. She said you've been seeing too much of each other lately, so on your last date she wore a blindfold.

_____ 5. His socks don't match.

_____ 6. His ears don't match.

_____ 7. He admits his socks don't match, but he claims it's because his feet don't match.

_____ 8. He whispered in your ear he'd never

been out with anyone like you before, but he didn't whisper that you're the first person he's ever been out with.

_____ 9. When you stop somewhere for a pizza, she insists on anchovies.

_____10. In school she's embarrassingly dumb.

_____11. In school she's embarrassingly smart.

_____12. While you were going with him he went out with another girl and didn't even bother to hide it — taking your sister out on nights he knew you'd be home!

_____13. He's forgetful. He forgets your birthday, your anniversary, your name.

_____14. He has this nervous habit of snapping his fingers.

_____15. He has this nervous habit of snapping your fingers.

_____16. Not only does she think your favorite book's really boring, she doesn't care for the way you colored the pictures, either.

_____17. He said he thought the picture on that ID card you carry in your purse is one of his favorite pictures of you, and it's not your ID card.

_____18. You planned to go to the costume party as Mork and Mindy, and when he showed up that night he was dressed as Mindy.

_____19. Not only does he step on your feet when you're dancing, he steps on them when you're not.

_____20. She said all she wanted was to go out just once with someone else before settling down to be your steady. That one time she went out, she agreed to marry the guy.

_____21. She told you she couldn't go out because she had to help her brother clean out the garage, but her family doesn't even have a driveway.

_____22. She's entirely too emotional — like the time you slammed the car door on her thumb and she didn't stop crying for over three minutes.

_____23. He's totally insensitive, like the time he slammed the car door on your thumb and he was all upset about the blood messing up his new wax job.

_____24. He likes peanut butter sandwiches spread with mustard.

_____25. He's so clumsy — every time he tries to hold your hand he drops it.

_____26. He can't keep his hands to himself, and he has trouble with his feet too.

_____27. He said he'd call you, and that was two years ago.

Having a Horrible Time, Wish You Weren't Here

There are times when a girl hasn't got any choice, she has to get rid of that not-so-special boy. *The BANANAS Dating Test and Survey* concluded that the best way is with a letter. Letters have the advantage of doing their dirty work totally removed from where the writer happens to be hiding. If you phone the poor guy, you may have to listen to a lot of pleading. And if you confront him face to face, you might feel some obligation to intervene should he decide to try to overdose on breath mints. No, there's no substitute for a letter if your goal is a nearly painless breakup. If you want a completely painless breakup, send the letter anonymously.

The following absolutely authentic letters were written by girls in our *BANANAS Dating Test* sample. Read the letters carefully, then answer the questions that follow.

Letter A

Dear John,
    This is one of the hardest letters I've ever had to write, and not just because my pen's nearly out of ink. I might as well just tell you, although I know we've had some good times together, a couple anyway, times I'll never for-

get if I live to be sixteen — it's over, finished, done! And I'm not doing this because you're not a nice guy, because you are. You're nice and you're sweet and you're always on time. In fact you're everything some girls could ask for, but I'm not that kind of girl. Call me fickle, call me shallow, just don't call me anymore.

No longer yours truly,
Ms. S. Smith

Letter B

Dear John,

I know what you're thinking, that this is going to be one of those horrible "Dear John" letters, John, and I want to assure you right away that it's *not!* In fact it's a letter about how much I really care for you and, because of that, how very much I'm going to miss you!

You see it all started when I got home from school Monday, and I found this big, long list of "Household Duties For Dottie" attached to the front of our new refrigerator with the ice maker. You can imagine how upset I was! Mom said she's just got to have more help around the house and, as much as I don't want to admit it, I think she's right! I *should* be doing more! I mean she's practically alone. It's just me, and Mom and Dad, and my two sisters, and my five older brothers. So I guess I won't be able to see you anymore because I've got all sorts of chores to do now — like today I have to clean out the septic tank, re-model the bathroom, and wash the dishes. I'm really going to miss you, but I'm also looking forward to this wonderful new opportunity in domestic engineering.

John, it's really been wonderful! It's all I can do to keep from falling apart right here at my desk, to hold back the rush of tears as I write this hated letter, and if it's got water spots on it, you'll know exactly where they came from! I think you know me well enough to know I'm not one of those sneaky girls who'd take a medicine dropper, fill it with tap water, and make spots all over a letter just to make her ex think she'd been crying.

Well, I've got to paint the house now. I'll probably be seeing you in the halls at school, but if I don't speak or even look at you, it'll just be because I'm too tired to open my mouth or focus my eyes.

With Warmest Last Regards,
Dot

Letter C

Dear John,
  GET LOST, CREEP!

  Ruby

Questions

1. Which letters worked? Did they work harder than Dottie?
2. Because of the notoriously slow postal system, which letter still hasn't been delivered?
3. Which letter arrived with postage due?
4. Which letter broke your heart, not when you saw it in this book, but when you received one just like it in your mailbox?
5. What's the proper way to address a letter like this — "Mr." or "Occupant"?

Letters from Homes

Dear BANANAS Dating Test:

I'm dating a 12th grader and he's promised to take me to the senior party. The problem is I'm only a sophomore. Does this mean I need more credits if I want to go to the senior party?

Confused Underclassman

Dear Confused Underclassman:

That's a really good question! Better check with your counselor!

Dear BANANAS Dating Test:

Your book says the boy should always "show the girl to her seat" in a movie theater. My only question is, why? I mean what difference does it make to the seat what the girl looks like? Am I right or what?

Confused Reader

Dear Confused Reader:

What.

Dear BANANAS Dating Test:

Thank you, oh, thank you! You've given me the courage to go on, even though nobody ever asks me to go anywhere!

Dear Stay-At-Home:
 It was nothing.

Dear BANANAS Dating Test:
 This is all your fault! Before I went out
last weekend, I read The BANANAS Dating
Test and Survey cover-to-cover and everything in between. In fact, I read the part
about how to kiss a girl good-night twice,
and I memorized those statistics on how
99% of the girls surveyed admitted they
kissed the boy good-night by at least the
third date. So, when I was out the other
night on the fourth date with this girl, I fig-
ured the odds were really with me, if you
know what I mean! But when I tried to kiss
her good-night she slapped me. She slapped
me so hard it dislocated my face. You may
think that's funny but, believe me, I'm not
laughing. It hurts too much. Since the problem's obviously not me, I figure it must be
the girls I ask out. What I want is for you to
send me a list of those you used in your
survey.

                    Puckered and Ready

Dear Puckered:
 Sure, just send us a self-addressed enve-
lope, and $10,000 for postage and handing.

Scoring The BANANAS Dating Test

You probably began this book on dating the same way you begin a date. When you leave for a date, you never know if you'll make the grade. With *The BANANAS Dating Test and Survey* there was never any question that you would make the grade. It was just a matter of which one.

You will find the answers for those tests that did not already have the answers included at the end of the test in the section immediately following these brief instructive remarks. If the answers to a particular test do not appear at the end of the test itself, or in the following section, then that was just one of those tests containing questions for which there aren't any answers.

Answer Section

Test #1: 1 — The left hand doesn't know whose hand the right hand's holding; 2 — Not if the little kid'll leave you alone for free; 3 — When the clock struck one; 4 — It's done with mirrors; 5 — Eastern Standard Time; 6 — Two rows in front of the first row of the balcony; 7 — Halfway between the white line and the yellow line; 8 — Three! One to hold the bulb and two to spin the stepladder!; 9 — There's one born every minute; 10 — It takes one to know one.

Test #2: See answers to Test #10 below.

Test #3: Better ask your father.

Test #4: Part A — $E = MC^2$; Part B — 10% benzoil peroxide.

Test #5: See answers to Test #7 below.

Test #6: Answers to this test will be made available sometime after the first of the year. The questions proved to be so difficult nobody on the staff was able to make out a key.

Test #7: 1 — Bismark, North Dakota; 2 — Bismark, East Dakota; 3 — Carson City, Nevada; 4 — Duluth, Minnesota; 5 — Paris, Kentucky; 6 — Niagara Falls, New York; 7 — Waldo, Ohio.

Test #8: 1 — Lollygagging; 2 — Spinning a bottle; 3 — Parking the car; 4 — Discussing the true meaning of life.

Test #9: True — if she'll buy it!

Figuring Out Your Grade

We want to make sure you get everything that's coming to you. Just do what you're told in these instructions, and we can practically guarantee you'll get yours!

Mark only those answers that are either right or wrong, leaving all the others alone. It'll be easier to go back and tally up your score if you mark the right answers with a C for "correct," and the wrong ones with OK for "OK, so I missed one!"

Start with Test #1. Add up all your right answers, then add up all your wrong answers and subtract the totals from the total number of questions asked which should be equal to the number of answers listed, plus seven to the first power, more or less. Repeat the same process for Tests #2, #3, #5 and so forth, right on through the alphabet. Don't forget to add in the fifteen point bonus you could be entitled to for being gullible enough to have read this far.

Add all of the scores from all of the tests you took to all of the scores from the tests you didn't take, forgot to take, simply couldn't take anymore, or got caught cheating on; divide that total by the total of the number of tests you could have taken had you taken any of this seriously.

How Do You Stack Up Against the Rest of the Entire Nation?

To compare your score with the national average, read down the left-hand column of Raw Scores until you find your own Raw Score. Then, when you're pretty well over the shock and humiliation, read across to the right-hand column to find out what it means.

The Bananas Dating Test and Survey National Average Scored Point Spread

Raw Score	Weight after Cooking	National Comparison: What it all Means
15	−12	99% of the American high school students who took these tests did better than you, and, on top of that, they had 43% fewer cavities!
24	−¼	You can count on spending another weekend home alone, unless you discover the only reason you got a score this high was you counted wrong. In that

case, you may not even be able to count on a weekend at home.

59	#9	If you were a fish, they'd throw you back.
66	355ml.	You should be proud of yourself. You actually made it all the way up the chart to where the category marked FAIL-URE starts!
72	375°	Good work! You can move to the head of your class, especially since it's a slow class.
88	AB+	This would be an excellent score if you were playing baseball. Unfortunately in real life this score puts you in the minor league.
100	¼lb.	There's no way you could have gotten a hundred on this battery of tests unless you just wrote any old answer that popped into your

head. There's really no excuse for taking these tests so lightly, in such a disgustingly irresponsible and immature manner. At the same time these comments should in no way detract from this impressive score! With *The BANANAS Dating Test and Survey* it's not whether you win or lose, it's whether you win.

| 103 | 6Gs | It's mathematically impossible to get this score! If you bungle a date the way you bungled figuring your average, you might as well plan now on spending the night of the big dance — possibly the rest of your life — trying to balance your checkbook. Forget about dating and get a hamster. |

The Official BANANAS Bio-Vac Computerless Dating Personality Profile

Are you dateless? Lonely? Of course you are, but here's some great news! Now, for the price of a stamp and check or money order for only $19.95, your good friends at **The BANANAS Computerless Dating Service** will be glad to match you up with that ideal person, the person of your dreams, a person just like you, except of the opposite sex. But before we do all this, and for practically no charge (after the low, one-time Follow-Up Fee of $10.00), you have to help us by completing the following Official BANANAS Bio-Vac Computerless Dating Personality Inventory.

(Fold, Bend, Spindle, Mutilate, or Tear Here)

Instructions: Answer each and every question. Be sure and read each item, preferably *before* marking down an answer. Circle A (AGREE); B (DISAGREE); C (DISAGREE-ABLE); D (TOO EMBARRASSED TO ANSWER); E (NONE OF YOUR DARN BUSINESS!) Write down the first answer that pops into your head and leave it. If you think twice about the questions, you might think twice about sending us your money.

Part I:

A B C D E   1. I believe in music.

A B C D E   2. I don't trust people with shifty eyes who sell used cars.

A B C D E   3. I prefer food that's edible.

A B C D E   4. I think it's okay for a young couple to hold hands after their fifteenth date, if both sets of parents give written permission.

A B C D E   5. The animal I most identify with is the sheep.

A B C D E   6. The animal I most identify with is the rat.

A B C D E   7. The animal I most identify with is my teddy bear.

A B C D E   8. I usually feel nervous and ill at ease if I'm caught in the middle of a hold-up.

A B C D E   9. I seldom get into arguments with other people unless I open my mouth.

A B C D E   10. I don't particularly like international terrorists.

A B C D E   11. I like to go to drive-in movies by myself.

A B C D E   12. When I'm wide awake I don't sleep very well.

A B C D E 13. I think having a certain balance in my life is very important. When something good happens, I look forward to something terrible happening to offset it.

A B C D E 14. If you want it to rain, all you have to do is go out and wash the car.

A B C D E 15. Everyone talks about the weather, but I believe there's a very small, select group of rich men actually doing something about it.

A B C D E 16. I don't think we're having as much fun today as people used to—at least I'm not.

A B C D E 17. When I'm not boring myself, you can usually find me boring others.

A B C D E 18. I don't approve of long hair and beards, especially on women.

A B C D E 19. If there's one thing I'm positive of, it's that I have a negative personality.

A B C D E 20. Every time the phone rings, I automatically assume it's a wrong number.

A B C D E   21. Every time the phone rings, it *is* a wrong number.

A B C D E   22. My dad can whip your dad any day of the week!

A B C D E   23. I believe there's a force in the universe greater than all of us, and it's out to get me.

A B C D E   24. Love is far more important than money except when you go shopping.

A B C D E   25. For every action there is an equal and opposite reaction.

A B C D E   26. When someone hits me really hard, it hurts.

A B C D E   27. I haven't had any problems with the opposite sex because none of them speak to me.

A B C D E   28. My favorite color is clear.

A B C D E   29. I can't say that I've had much respect for the people who've stood me up, nor have I thought very highly of the ones I've stood up.

A B C D E   30. The only time I snore is when I'm asleep.

A B C D E   31. I never answer questionnaires like this honestly.

Part II: To Be Completed by Boys Only

A B C D E   1. I don't believe in putting any pressure on a girl, so if she signals that she doesn't want to kiss good-night, I wait almost a full two minutes before trying again.

A B C D E   2. I wouldn't walk across the street to see Brooke Shields.

A B C D E   3. I'd run.

A B C D E   4. I like to climb trees.

A B C D E   5. When there aren't any trees to climb, I climb the walls.

A B C D E   6. Your typical girl out on a date wears so much perfume that the boy's new cologne just hasn't got a chance.

Part III: To Be Completed by Girls Only

A B C D E   1. I don't trust men who wear after shave lotion behind their ears.

A B C D E   2. I don't trust the rest of them either.

A B C D E   3. I wouldn't walk across the street to see Robert Redford.

A B C D E   4. I'd fly!

Mailing Instructions:

First, make out your check or money order. You must include the first payment of $29.95, plus the nominal charge of $15.95 for processing and handling, or one convenient time-saving payment of $129.99 for the semi-complete package. If paid separately, the total would be $35.95 plus tax and deposit, but when you consider all the time spent writing out the checks, putting them in the envelopes, addressing them, figuring your time to be worth at least $64.78 an hour, you enjoy a total savings of $3.10! And after you've sent us the money, you'll never see it again which means you'll have one less thing to worry about!

Remove the completed Personality Profile from this book. PLEASE DO NOT SEND THE ENTIRE BOOK. WE READ IT ONCE AND ONCE IS PLENTY!

ABOUT THE AUTHOR

Joe Arthur, a renowned expert, has been a writer longer than anyone cares to remember. He began by learning how to hold a pencil, then, how to hold a typewriter. Arthur joined the staff of his school newspaper while in only his fifth year of high school.

Arthur now writes for *BANANAS* magazine, and in his spare time he is a history and government teacher and second-period hall monitor at Whetstone High School in Columbus, Ohio. In addition to teaching, Arthur coaches track and cross-country. His biggest athletic thrill to date was the day the entire school turned out to hang him in effigy. (The dummy even looked a little like him, he admits, except that Arthur usually has more straw sticking out of his shirt.)

Arthur lives in a house with his two daughters, one wife, one dog, two cats, and two fish. He suspects there might be a mouse out in the garage.